Write Novels Fast: Writing Faster With Art Journaling

Shéa MacLeod

Write Novels Fast:
Writing Faster With Art Journaling
Copyright © 2017 Shéa MacLeod
All rights reserved.
Printed in the United States of America.

The characters and events portrayed in this book are fictitious. Any similarity to real persons, living or dead, is coincidental and not intended by the author.

No part of this book may be reproduced, or stored in a retrieval system, or transmitted in any form or by any means, electronic, mechanical, photocopying, recording, or otherwise, without express written permission of the publisher.

Chapter 1

Why A Journal?

Once upon a time. That's the way most stories start, right? Except this one doesn't. This one starts with yelling, screaming, a little bit of crying, a laptop through the window...

I always wanted to be a writer. From the first time I picked up a book, I knew what I wanted in life. I wanted to tell stories. My heroes were authors. My drug of choice the written word. I've been known to fondly caress the blank pages of a notebook....but I digress.

You see, while I knew I wanted to be a writer, actually writing something was a whole different ball of wax. So to speak. The method of writing—of finishing a novel—it escaped me entirely.

My first attempt at a novel was a romantic suspense. I totally pantsed the whole thing. No plotting. Just flying by the seat of my pants, making things up as I went along. What resulted was a horrifying, melodramatic hodge podge worthy of the worst Spaghetti Western.

Then I heard a very famous mystery writer give a talk (Okay, it was Janet Evanovich). She used the story board method. I can't draw to save my life, but I do see scenes from books much as one sees trailers for movies. So, I tried my own version. Instead of creating story boards for scenes, I just wrote the scenes as I saw them, when I saw them. Sounds awesome, right?

You would be wrong. What I ended up with was a huge pile of disjointed (but awesome) scenes which wouldn't fit together no matter how hard I tried. I think it took seven years of waiting for magical inspiration to hit before I finished the first (truly scary) draft.

And then came *Kissed by Darkness*. I spent ten years working on that thing. I tried pantsing. I tried story boards. I tried one of those outlines like you did in school as a kid. The horror of such detailed planning stifled my creativity. Nothing worked. Everything was awful. The world ended. Zombie apocalypse...

And then I stumbled on an article about Neil Gaiman and how he writes. I can't for the life of me find the original article, but I remember a picture of him up on a camel (You can find plenty of interesting articles by Googling "Neil Gaiman Journal"). He explained that he plots his novel and writes his first draft entirely by hand in a notebook. One of the reasons being that he doesn't have to mess about with a laptop when travelling (particularly to exotic places where there aren't a lot of electrical outlets, such as the backs of camels). Something inside me sparked.

And so I created my own amalgam of pantsing, plotting, outlining, and storyboarding. All in the form of an art journal.

Glue! Scissors! Colored pens!

The clouds broke apart. Sunlight shone. Angels sang.

And I finished *Kissed by Darkness* within six months. *Kissed by Fire* followed in three. And *Dragon Warrior* in under two. I'd found it. My method. It might be nutty, but it worked for me.

Now, I don't handwrite first drafts (Can you imagine the writer's cramps?). But I do plot everything in my journals. I know there are programs that let you do something similar to what I do on your computer, but that doesn't work for me. I need to *feel* the paper, the pens. I need to physically write out the details. Plus it lets me indulge my love of cute journals.

A couple years ago I began art journaling, as well. I love being able to express my artistic side while having absolutely no artistic ability whatsoever. And I've applied many of those things I've learned into my plotting journals.

People often ask me how I write so many books in so short a time and keep everything straight (I've published over 35 titles in under 6 years). I show them my journals. They're often fascinated. Sometimes inspired.

Recently I taught a good friend of mine this method. She's a total pantser. She went from writing a single book every year or two, to writing four books in one year. If this method can more than quadruple her writing speed, imagine what it could do for yours!

As writers we're always evolving, changing, and so are our methods. Over time, mine certainly has. Hopefully you take away something valuable from my method. Not everything I'm going to share will work for you. Take what works, throw the rest out.

Now get out the glue a scissors and let's journal!

Chapter 2

To Outline Or Not To Outline

Your plotting journal can be as detailed and beautiful or as simple and basic as you want it to be. A writer friend of mine has created some gorgeous art journals for her books in order to gain inspiration. With paint and inspirational quotes and other goodies she's created a true work of art reflective of her novel. It's a fantastic way to get creative juices flowing when you're stuck on a project.

My journals, however, tend to be much simpler. More basic. I'm not using them as much for inspiration (although there's an element of that) as I am to get the job of plotting done. To give me a guideline when I begin writing. And, of course, to create a reference for things like characters, locations, and so on.

I have created a basic list of supplies you'll need to get you started on your plotting journal:

- Blank journal (I prefer something with a spine and lined paper. Some prefer ring binder style as they stay open easier.)
- Character/location/inspirational images
- Stick glue (You can use rubber cement, but it's a hot mess and stinks.)
- Scissors
- Ballpoint pen

In addition, you might want to get some other fun supplies such as:

- Colored markers
- Colored ballpoint pens
- Highlighters
- Washi tape
- Post-It Notes (in several colors)
- Label printer (Or fun labels you can write on)
- Other art supplies you want to play with.

First of all, let's throw the word "outline" right out of our lexicon. It dredges up images of Roman numerals and hours spent bent over a paper trying to diagram paragraphs. Blergh. Who wants that? It takes all the fun out of writing, in my opinion.

I know that there are some out there, however, who *love* to plot in minute detail. It works for them. And that's okay. My method can work for you regardless of if you're a plotter or a pantser.

What I love about plot journals is that it allows me to create a guide. A sort of framework which keeps me on the straight and narrow while allowing my creativity free reign. And I can change the road maps whenever I want, so if the story veers left when I planned for a slow right turn, well, there's room for that.

There are three major components to the plotting journal:
1. Overall plotting (character profiles, overall story notes, etc.)
2. Chapter details (or what some call an "outline")
3. Rewrites and Edit notes

Of course, those sections are further broken down, but we'll get to that. For now, pens to the read. Let's get started!

Chapter 3

Inspiration, Characters, and All That Jazz

The first section of my plotting journals always starts with notes on the overall story. These are general vague ideas such as main character name, location, and a couple words on plot. The first little spark of an idea. I call this **Plot Notes**.

Usually this is written in plain black ink. Sometimes it gets tweaked. Sometimes it doesn't. Sometimes it gets outlined in Washi tape. Because Washi tape is fun. Sometimes it doesn't because I'm in a hurry.

Other times I create a pocket (such as in the image below) where I can tuck bits of paper on which I've written random notes. That way everything is nice and tidy in one place. Plus, it's cute. I mean, come on, that little skull pocket? Don't you love it?

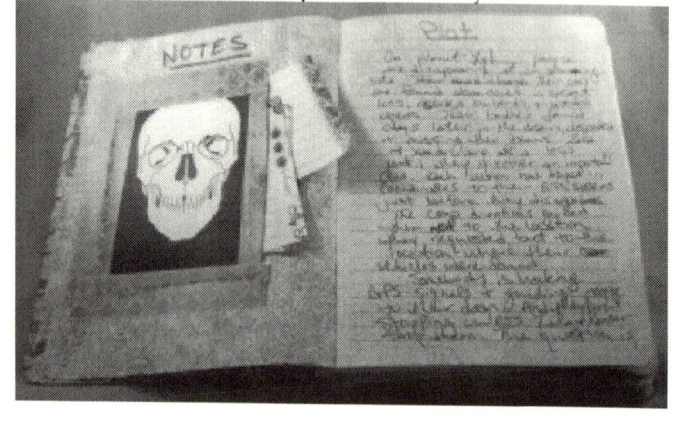

In my first Lady Rample novel (Which is in its early stages of plotting as of this writing), I simply listed the title, series title, book number, and the meaning of Lady Rample's surname:

Lady Rample Steps Out
Lady Rample Mysteries - Book One
"Rample = **For a female to render a male helpless with a kind of coldly elusive sexuality.**"

And that's all I've got. Because we're still in early stages. However, *Mistwalker*, the third book in the Sunwalker Saga: Witchblood series, reads more like this:

After being plagued by images of murder, Veri sets out to find a rogue psychic and serial killer. What she doesn't know (initially), is that he knows she's been watching and is hunting her, too.

When a dragon ends up dead at the hand of a rogue psychic, Drago (King of the Dragons) sends one of his enforcers (Vane) to hunt the psychic and bring him to justice, dragon style...

And so on. It's almost a blurb, really, but much longer and with more specific details to remind me where I'm going (Not that I stick with it 100%, but that's another story). Sometimes I add in a couple inspirational images. For instance, in *The Stiff in the Study* I included an image of Flavel House, an important location in the novel and the inspiration for the plot.

This is also where I include world building information. Everything from swear words (often written on index cards for easy reference) to drawings of vampire hunting weapons.

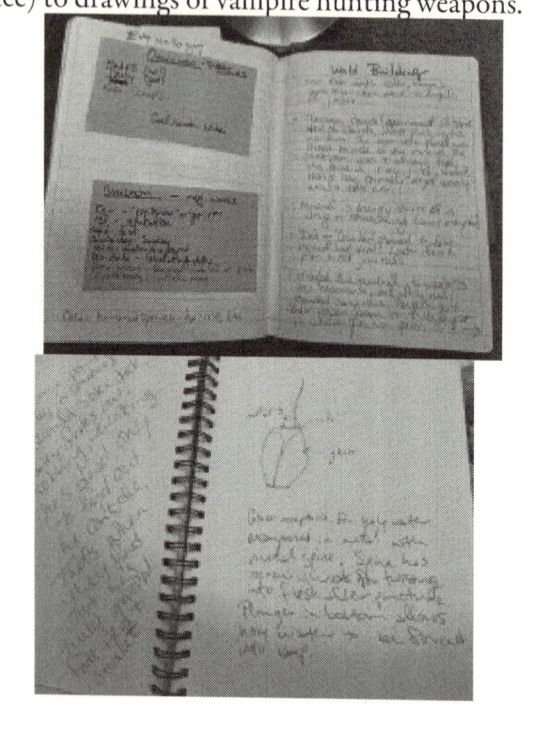

I find these notes useful mostly in the earliest stages of plotting a novel and rarely refer to them afterward. (Except for the world building, of course. I reference that a lot.) They're more inspiration and general direction than anything else. At least for me.

Depending on the book, I can have several pages of "inspirational material," or just one. Some stories just need a little more nudging than others to get the creative juices flowing.

You might find this section more or less useful depending on how your mind works and where you are in planning your project. You might have only a single, simple page as I do, or you might fill half a dozen pages with images, words, and phrases that inspire you. That is the joy of plot journaling! Whatever works for you, do that.

The second section within **Overall Plotting** contains the **Character Profiles**. Frankly, these are the most fun for me because I get to meet all these fascinating new characters. And hunt for images of hot guys online. (Kidding. But only a little.)

Within **Character Profiles** I usually break down the characters into three subgroups:

1. Main Characters
2. Secondary Characters
3. Tertiary Characters

Since I write in series, most of my Main Characters (MCs) remain main characters throughout the series (although there are a couple series where the MCs in one book become Secondaries in the next book and vice versa). Obviously in situations where the MCs remain the same throughout a series, the first journal in the series has the most detail on those characters.

The MCs each get their own two page spread (or more as necessary). This is where I pull out my colored markers and go to town! Names in bright letters across the top of the page. Stunning photos (printed from the internet) pasted willy nilly. And in black ink I include details such as age, basic stats, pertinent background, favorite drinks, and so on. Information that makes my characters come alive.

These pages get added to randomly as the characters evolve. Additions are usually made in the same color, but changes are made in a second color, such as red, so I can see them more easily.

For instance, in the plot journal for *Kissed by Darkness*, Morgan Bailey's original name was Bailey Morgan. It was changed for reasons.

In Lady Rample, I included images of a 1930s Mercedes Roadster (Lady R's car of choice) and pictures of Katherine Hepburn and Evan Rachel Wood (Inspirations for Lady R). In the first Viola Roberts book I included images of Melissa McCarthy, who inspired Viola, and Oded Fehr, who inspired her love interest, Lucas Salvatore.

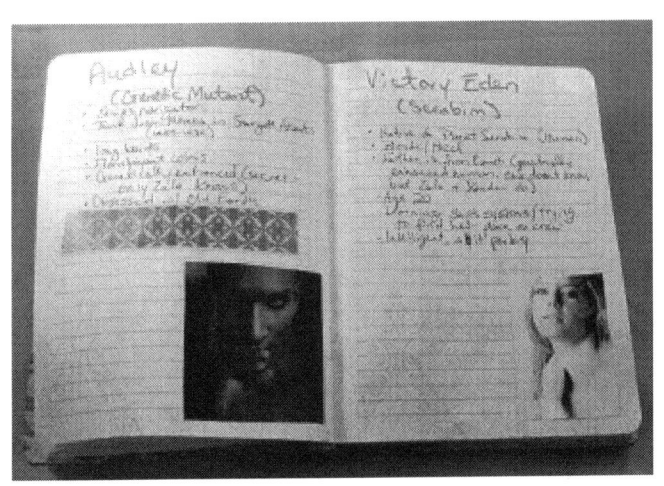

Before I continue, a note on images:

While I highly recommend legally purchasing stock photos from a reputable source for any sort of promo you plan to do, swiping images of celebrities to use in your personal plotting journal is perfectly fine. They're for your personal use, so grab what appeals to you. Just don't try to make a teaser out of it or use your journal as a promotional scheme (all the images in this book were legally purchased from a stock photo site or are ones I took myself).

Onward...

Secondary characters, particularly the important ones, get a single page spread. Cheryl in the Viola Roberts books has her own page and image (Halle Berry). She's Viola's best friend and appears, at least briefly, in all the books. She's important, and therefore requires more information.

Other secondaries share a page and get a short paragraph each. Such as Viola's mother. Or Jason Wu in *Dragon Mage*, who is an important secondary character, but appears only briefly.

Tertiary characters just get listed on a page together, maybe with a word or two about who they are or what they look like. This is mostly so I don't forget their names (or how I spelled them). For instance, Queen Boudicca in the Dragon Wars series. So far she's been mentioned in two books, but she's never appeared "on screen," as it were.

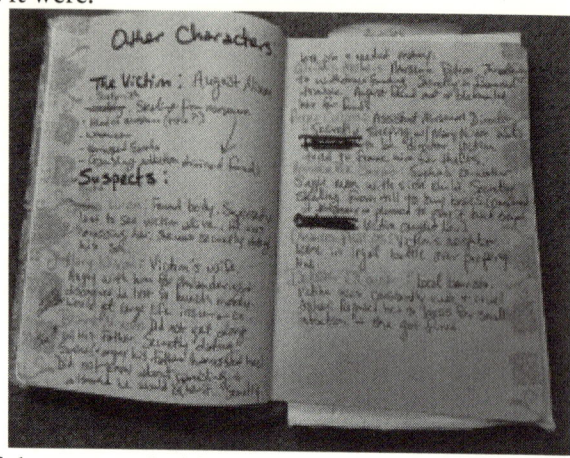

In each of these I use the black/red (or black/pink) ink method so I know when I've changed something. The change stands out. And believe me, I change a lot of things as I'm writing. This stuff isn't set in stone!

All of this is reference. I write what's important to me. I include as few or as many images as I need. If you need six pages on your MC, that's totally fine. If you want images for each of your secondaries and tertiaries, that's fine, too. Just don't let the creation of **Character Profiles** get in the way of writing those characters' stories.

At the back of the **Character Profiles** I leave a page or two for final notes. This is where I often use more Washi tape. Because one can never have too much Washi tape.

This is usually where I slap more involved ideas for the plot, often written on Post-its. For instance, in Lady Rample I currently have two sticky notes. One reads:

Attends burlesque - patron or dancer murdered.

Include jazz club/speakeasy sort of place.
The second contains notes on who the possible killer will be. I won't share that. Spoilers!

Below is an example of these pages from one of the Viola Roberts books. You can see the hand drawn graph on the left page of how I figured out who the killer would be.

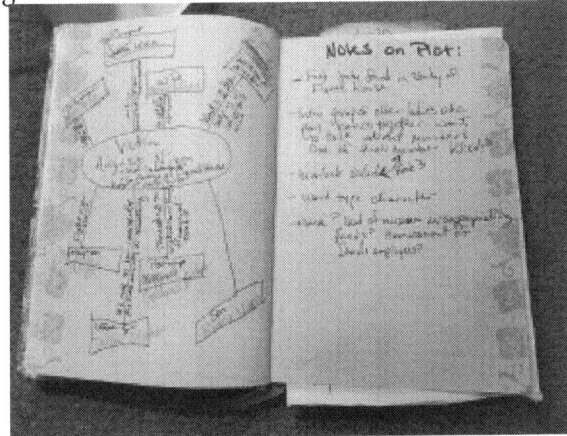

Again, make as much or as little of this as works for you. You might not need it at all. You might need twelve pages. I've literally done both. For me, the need varies from project to project. Don't let yourself get trapped in the minutiae of "I must do this or that." This journal is meant to work for *you*. Not the other way around.

And for goodness sake, make it fun!

Chapter 4

Nitty Gritty

Now we get down to the nitty gritty. The real meat and potatoes of this whole art journal. This is where we get down the details of the plot.

If you're a plotter, this should be easy for you. More or less. If you're a pantser, you might be wondering why you should do this at all. Here's why:

Giving yourself a road map will keep you from getting lost. You don't have to see the whole forest, just the windy path through the trees. Knowing where you're going can keep you on point, allowing you to write much faster. And having a map to refer to, will help keep you headed in the right direction. You don't have to know every little plot point, you just need a general direction.

So, instead of sitting blankly in front of the computer for hours on end, you know where you're going. And instead of writing randomly, hoping something will pop out at you, you have a general point at which to aim.

Here's what I do:

In a bright, colored marker, I write the chapter number at the top of each page. Each chapter gets a page front and back. That's it. *I highly recommend this even if you're a plotter.* Why? Because plotters have a tendency to get wrapped up in the minutiae of their plots and not sit their butts down and write.

The point of this whole thing is to *write fast*. Get out that first draft no matter how rough. This is not the Sistine Chapel we're painting here. This is a first draft. It doesn't have to be pretty. You can fix it later.

Once again for those in the back:

You can fix it later.

That's the point of rewrites. *This* section is about getting those words on the page.

The art journal for my first published book, *Kissed by Darkness,* was pretty detailed (as you can see below). Hey, it was my first book. I didn't know what I was doing. As I've gotten my process nailed down, my "outlines" have become increasingly simple.

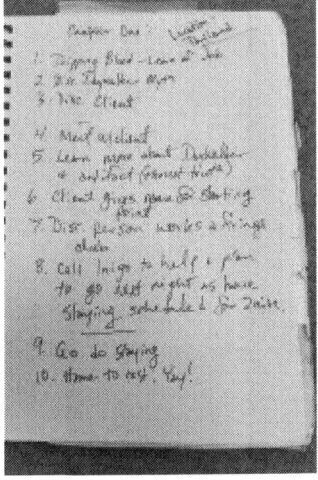

Nowadays I do a maximum of four plot points per chapter. You don't need more than that. For instance, in *Dragon Mage,* I've got only one or two plot points per chapter. They're short chapters in a short book. I don't need more than that.

The Chapter One "outline" looks like this:

- Ben is sent on trading mission to the Badlands.
- During trip, convoy is attacked by "bandits." Ben is injured.

That's literally it. And that's all I needed. That was enough to visualize those scenes in my head, sit down at the computer, and start banging them out.

But what happens when things change?

Glad you asked. Because things *did* change in *Dragon Mage*. I decided that starting off with Ben getting orders was boring and totally unnecessary. So, I started it off with a *bang*! Right in the middle of a dragon attack (In case you're wondering, the Dragon Wars series is about a post-apocalyptic world with dragons, so this totally makes sense). Then we find out why Ben's in the badlands getting attacked by dragons in the first place. He still gets attacked by bandits, because why not, but not until chapter two.

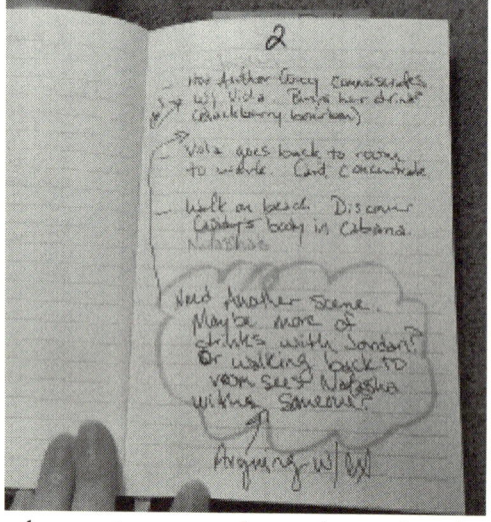

Again, adding changes in a secondary color makes them pop. It's easier for reference.

So, basically, you just go through chapter by chapter and add the plot points and sub-plot points as necessary. You can change things whenever you need to, but this is the initial road map.

"But what if I don't know what's going to happen in chapter fifteen?"

Again, glad you asked. Leave it blank. Yeah, I said it. *Leave it blank.*

Often I'm not sure how many chapters a book will have. I've got a good guess, but it's only that. A guess. I know what's going to happen in the first few chapters. And I know what's going to happen in the last few. And I know a few things in between.

So, I write what I know in my journal and leave the rest blank. Later, once I've written the first few chapters and maybe brain stormed with a friend, I go back in fill in the rest.

It's okay to have blank pages. It's okay not to be sure. Because more often than not, once you start down that path, the rest of the journey becomes clear.

"But how do you know for sure that this information will fall in that specific chapter?"

The answer? I don't. And you know what? It doesn't matter! Just take that marker, scribble out the three in Chapter Three and make it a two. Or whatever.

The outline is merely a road map and there are lots of options to get from Point A to Point B. The outline helps you get there. It isn't made of concrete.

Liberating, don't you think?

There is another method of organization I've used for outlining. I don't use it super often and find it most useful for mysteries where I've got a lot of plot threads running around. I definitely used it in *Dragon Mage* where I had the main plot between Ben and Bella (including a romance, kidnapping, and dragon fighting), and a subplot involving a coup back in China Town (between two other characters, Angel and Takei).

For each plot line within your story, use a different color ballpoint pen. For instance, let's say the main plot is the romance between Ben and Bella, their interactions and so on. That could be in black ink. It's probably going to have the most writing anyway.

Then you've got the coup back in China Town. Go for red. Because murder!

Then there are the interactions between Ben and his mentor, Jason. Those could be in blue.

And finally, there's Bella's sister, Lola, and her shenanigans. Those are in green.

Corrections can be made in another color such as pink or orange.

And there you go. All the colors!

Chapter 5

All the Rewrites!

The final section of my plotting art journal are the **Rewrites** and **Edits**. And this is where things get a bit wild.

While I'm still writing the first draft, I keep notes under the heading **"Rewrites"** on things I realize I need to expand upon, add, or change. For instance, in *Mistwalker* I realized Veri had done almost no spellcasting in the entire story. And yet, she's a witch. So, that seems like a failing. My rewriting notes included an idea on how she could help a client using her magic. Voila! Problem solved.

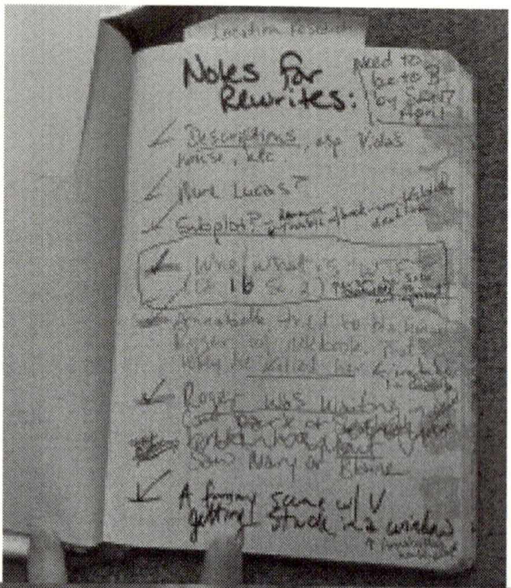
Notes for Rewrites:

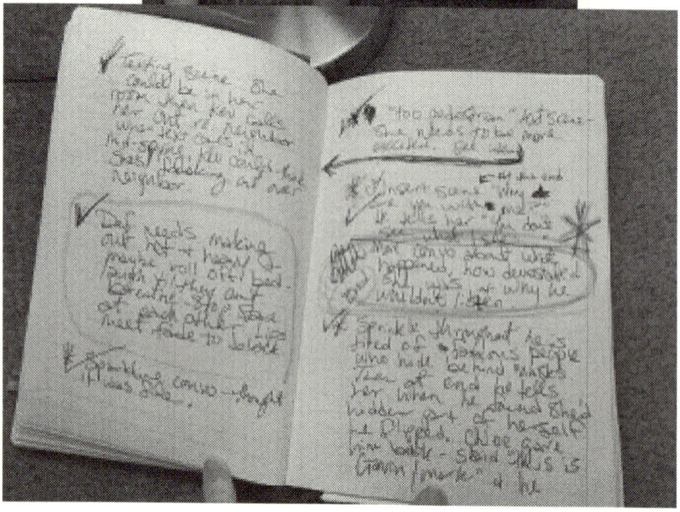

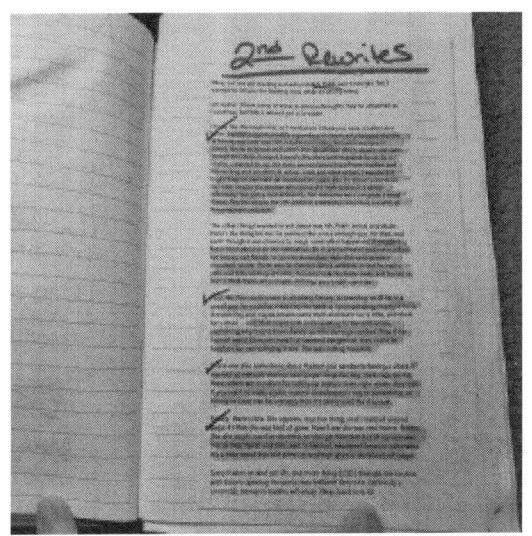

A second note regarded some details in the first two books. I couldn't remember specifics of certain characters' histories, so I needed to go back and check those manuscripts.

DO NOT ACT ON THESE NOTES!

At least, not while you're writing the first draft. This will only slow you down. If you think of something that needs changed or added, write it in your **Rewrites** section. Don't act on it. Wait. And when the first draft is finished, go back and work on these items during rewrites.

Once the rewrites are done and the book is off to your editor, create a final heading **"Edits."** Similar to **"Rewrites,"** this is where you keep notes for things to fix during edits. Usually your editor will include those notes within your manuscript, but sometimes they like to give ideas separately. Or sometimes while speaking to a critique partner or thinking about your manuscript, you realize something needs to change.

In *Mistwalker* I realized that Veri and Vane's chemistry was...lacking. I seriously needed to ramp up the heat between the two of them. I also reworked some of Vane's backstory and realized I needed to go back and tweak some other parts of the story to reflect that.

This is where, once again, color comes in. I don't do rewrites or edits in order, necessarily. I usually do the easiest ones first and tick them off as I go. Then I go back to the harder ones, the ones that need more thought and a bigger chunk of work.

This can result in me missing an editing point. So, I highlight the heck out of things to make sure I go back and hit anything I skipped.

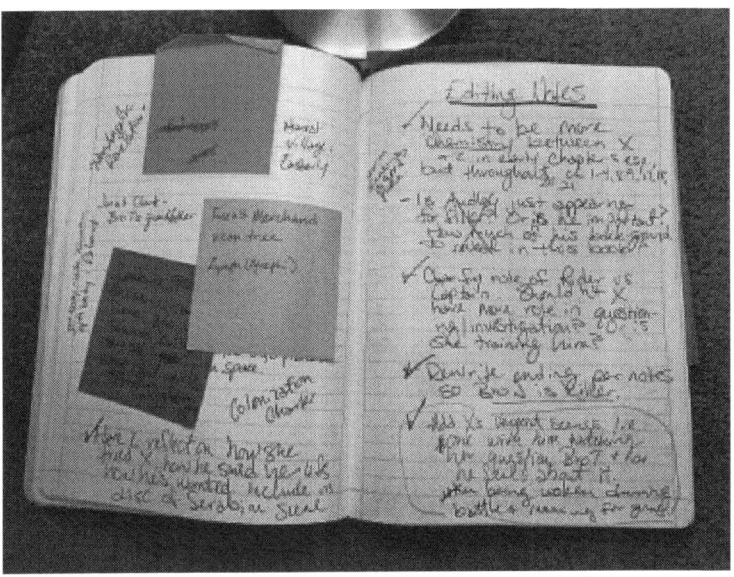

Once all the items are checked, I know I've finished editing and the manuscript is ready for the next step. The art journal gets tucked on the shelf, ready for future reference, or additional notes regarding audiobooks, promotion, etc.

Chapter 6

Final Thoughts...

And that's it for art journal plotting. It's fun, it's easy, it's not expensive, and it's a simple way to keep yourself organized and create a future reference for series books. Not to mention the increase in writing speed, especially when coupled with sprinting (you can learn more about that on my blog: https://sheamacleod.wordpress.com/).

Things to remember about your art journal plotting:

1. Keep it simple.
2. Make it work for you.
3. Don't get bogged down in plotting and forget to write!
4. You don't have to know every detail.
5. Have fun!

Happy art journaling!

Want More Writing Tips?

Sign up for Shéa MacLeod's newsletter at: http://www.subscribepage.com/o0m5q9

Note from the Author

Thank you for reading. If you enjoyed this book, I'd appreciate it if you'd help others find it so they can enjoy it too.

- Lend it: This e-book is lending-enabled, so feel free to share it with your friends, readers' groups, and discussion boards.

- Review it: Let other potential readers know what you liked or didn't like about the story.

Book updates can be found at www.sheamacleod.com

About Shéa MacLeod

Shéa MacLeod is the author of the international bestselling paranormal series, Sunwalker Saga, as well as the award nominated cozy mystery series Viola Roberts Cozy Mysteries. She has dreamed of writing novels since before she could hold a crayon. She totally blames her mother.

She resides in the leafy green hills outside Portland, Oregon where she indulges in her fondness for strong coffee, Ancient Aliens reruns, lemon curd, and dragons. She can usually be found at her desk dreaming of ways to kill people (or vampires). Fictionally speaking, of course.

Fiction by Shéa MacLeod

Sunwalker Saga
Kissed by Darkness
Kissed by Fire
Kissed by Smoke
Kissed by Moonlight
Kissed by Ice
Kissed by Blood
Kissed by Destiny
Sunwalker Saga: Soulshifter Trilogy
Fearless
Haunted
Soulshifter
Sunwalker Saga: Witchblood
Spellwalker
Deathwalker
Mistwalker
Dragon Wars
Dragon Warrior
Dragon Lord
Dragon Goddess
Green Witch
Dragon Corps
Dragon Mage
Dragon Wars- Three Complete Novels Boxed Set
Cupcake Goddess Novelettes
Be Careful What You Wish For
Nothing Tastes As Good
Soulfully Sweet
A Stich in Time
Omicron ZX
Omicron Zed-X: An Omicron ZX prequel
A Rage of Angels
Viola Roberts Cozy Mysteries
The Corpse in the Cabana
The Stiff in the Study

The Poison in the Pudding
The Body in the Bathtub
The Venom in the Valentine
The Remains in the Rectory

Don't miss out!

Click the button below and you can sign up to receive emails whenever Shéa MacLeod publishes a new book. There's no charge and no obligation.

Sign Me Up!

https://books2read.com/r/B-A-EJM-GVQN

BOOKS 2 READ

Connecting independent readers to independent writers.

Also by Shéa MacLeod

Cupcake Goddess
Be Careful What You Wish For
Nothing Tastes As Good
Soulfully Sweet
A Stitch In Time (A Cupcake Goddess Novelette)

Dragon Wars
Dragon Warrior
Dragon Lord
Dragon Goddess
Green Witch
Dragon Corps
Dragon Wars - Three Complete Novels Boxed Set

Notting Hill Diaries
Kissing Frogs
Kiss Me, Chloe
Kiss Me, Stupid
Kissing Mr. Darcy
To Kiss A Prince

Omicron ZX
A Rage of Angels

Omicron ZX - Prequel
Omicron Zed-X

Sunwalker Saga
Kissed by Blood
Kissed by Destiny

Sunwalker Saga: Soulshifter Trilogy
Haunted
Soulshifter
Fearless

Sunwalker Saga: Witchblood
Spellwalker
Deathwalker
Mistwalker

Viola Roberts Cozy Mysteries
The Corpse in the Cabana
The Stiff in the Study
The Poison in the Pudding
The Body in the Bathtub
The Venom in the Valentine
The Remains in the Rectory

Standalone
Ride the Dragon: A Paranormal/Science Fiction Boxed Set
Angel's Fall
Write Novels Fast: Writing Faster Through Art Journaling

Watch for more at sheamacleod.com.

Made in the USA
Middletown, DE
03 June 2021